SUPERMAN

AND THE LEGION OF SUPER-HEROES

READER SERVICES

CUSTOMER SERVICE IN THE UK AND REPUBLIC OF IRELAND
How to continue your collection:
Subscribe online at www.hachettepartworks.com/dccollection
For UK call 0345 155 6374, or for ROI call (01) 9079762
(Calls are charged at your local rate from a landline)

Back issues: Visit our online shop at: www.hachettepartworks.com to purchase specials and any back
issues you may have missed to ensure you have a complete collection. Issues will be priced as normal
with an additional P&P cost of £2.50. Free P&P on orders over £30.

CUSTOMER SERVICE, SUBSCRIPTIONS & BACK ORDERS IN OVERSEAS MARKETS
Australia – email: customer_service_aus@hachette-service.com or alternatively call (02) 8378 7931
New Zealand – email: info@mycollectables.co.nz or alternatively call (09) 928 4493
South Africa – email: southafrica@hachette-service.com or alternatively call 0027 101095300
Published by Hachette Partworks Ltd, 4th Floor, Jordan House, 47 Brunswick Place, London N1 6EB
Distributed in the UK and Republic of Ireland by Marketforce.
© 2022 Hachette Partworks Ltd

Collection Editor: Nick Jones
Design: Amazing15
Printed in Spain
ISSN 2634-0143
ALL RIGHTS RESERVED

CONTENTS

INTRODUCTION

Like many of the stories in the *DC Heroes & Villains Collection*, *Superman and the Legion of Super-Heroes* has been carefully selected both to demonstrate the interconnectedness of the DC Universe, and to work as a stand-alone story in its own right. Certain plot strands herein stretch back to another Geoff Johns-written volume in the collection, *Justice League of America: The Lightning Saga* (and even to the *Justice Society of America* volume *The Next Age*), and forward to *Legion of 3 Worlds* (which also acts as a sequel to yet another Johns-written *DC Heroes & Villains Collection* story, *Green Lantern: The Sinestro Corps War*).

Anyone wishing to follow those strands will find their reading experience richly enhanced as a result, but *Superman and the Legion of Super-Heroes* works just as well in its own right as a first-rate Superman/Legion story. It's also notable for marking the start of a creative collaboration

at DC that has proved remarkably enduring. Geoff Johns and Gary Frank had briefly worked together prior to this tale, on a couple of issues of Marvel's *Avengers* in 2003, but it was when Frank joined Johns at DC in 2007 that their collaborations stepped up a level. Following the joint tenure on *Action Comics* that began with *Superman and the Legion of Super-Heroes*, the pair retold the Man of Steel's beginnings in *Superman: Secret Origins* (2009–10); reimagined the Dark Knight's early career in three *Batman: Earth One*

> It was when Frank joined Johns at DC in 2007 that their collaborations stepped up a level.

4

graphic novels (2012–21); revitalised Shazam in back-up stories in *Justice League* (2012–13); and deconstructed the entire DC Universe in *Doomsday Clock* (2018–20).

Frank discusses their fruitful partnership at the back of this book in a brand new interview, while for his part, Johns has been similarly effusive over the years, not least in the early days of their DC collaborations, when they were working on *Action*

Comics. Speaking to Comic Book Resources at the start of 2008, Johns said of Frank: "He's got this great kind of modern Curt Swan kind of look to his Superman and Curt Swan is my favourite Superman artist ever. So to have Gary on the book with me and getting those pages and discussing the character with him and bouncing ideas off of him, it's really a great partner to have on the very first superhero title." **DC**

GEOFF JOHNS is the multi-award-winning writer of numerous bestselling comic books, including *JSA*, *Green Lantern: Rebirth*, *Action Comics*, *The Flash: Rebirth*, *Blackest Night*, *Brightest Day*, *Flashpoint*, *Aquaman*, *Justice League*, *Shazam!*, *Doomsday Clock*, *Batman: Three Jokers*, and the *Batman: Earth One* graphic novel series. Having started out in the mid-1990s as an assistant to *Superman* director Richard Donner, Johns began writing comics in 1999, launching the series *Stars and S.T.R.I.P.E.*, which featured future Stargirl Courtney Whitmore. His film and TV careers have continued in parallel to his comics work, his credits including writing and producing for *Arrow*, *Aquaman*, *The Flash*, *Stargirl*, and *Wonder Woman 1984*.

GARY FRANK began his career in his native UK in 1991, drawing short stories for *Doctor Who Magazine* and *Toxic!* By the end of 1992, he was working for Marvel in the US, pencilling covers and then interiors for *Incredible Hulk*. His first assignments for DC came in 1996, with a *Birds of Prey: Black Canary/Oracle* one-shot and a new series of *Supergirl*, after which he became the regular artist of WildStorm's *Gen 13*. His projects since then have included *Kin*, *Midnight Nation*, and *Supreme Power*, and at DC *Superman: Secret Origin*, the *Batman: Earth One* graphic novel series, and *Doomsday Clock*. The latter three projects were created in collaboration with Geoff Johns, with whom Frank launched the Image series, *Geiger*, in 2021.

ACTION COMICS #858 COVER
ART BY GARY FRANK

THEN *EARTH* IS OUR ONLY HOPE.

THAT'S WHAT I'M TALKING ABOUT, KENT.

YOU NEED TO MAKE SOME FRIENDS YOUR OWN AGE. WHY, YOU'VE BEEN HERE WHAT-- THREE YEARS?

TEN, MR. WHITE.

AND YET I HAVEN'T SEEN YOU MAKE A SINGLE FRIEND OUTSIDE OF JAMES OLSEN! SOME WOULD CALL THAT STRANGE OR UNHEALTHY, BUT YOU KNOW WHAT I CALL IT?

BAD LUCK?

A LACK OF SELF-CONFIDENCE!

DO YOU SEE THAT? WHAT IS IT?

YOU'RE A HELL OF A REPORTER, BUT YOU NEED TO LEARN HOW TO REACH OUT TO PEOPLE.

IT'S COMING THIS WAY!

TELL A JOKE. TALK ABOUT SPORTS. HELL, SHARE YOUR MOTHER'S APPLE PIE RECIPE!

IT'S AN ALIEN INVASION!

RELATE TO PEOPLE!

YOU DO KNOW HOW TO RELATE TO PEOPLE, DON'T YOU, KENT?

HELP!

KENT?!

ACTUALLY, MR. WHITE, I THINK THERE MIGHT'VE BEEN SOME ONIONS ON MY CHEESEBURGER AFTER ALL.

AND YOU GOTTA LEARN HOW TO STOP BEING SO SENSITIVE!

Hmph...

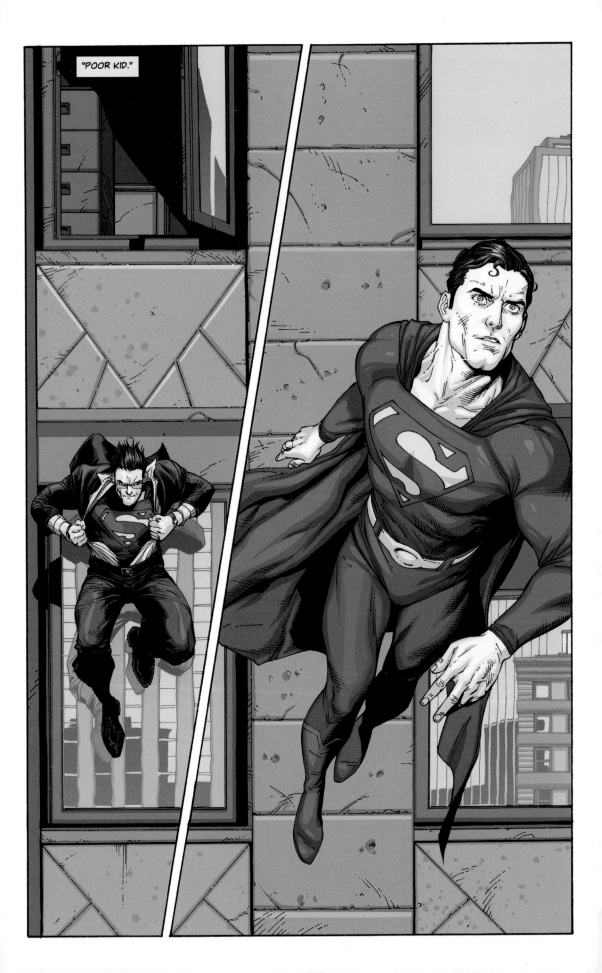

HE TOLD ME HE COULDN'T PLAY FOOTBALL BECAUSE HE DIDN'T WANT TO BREAK HIS GLASSES.

HE'S AFRAID OF *EVERYTHING.* ESPECIALLY *GIRLS.*

HAHAHA HAHA!

HE'S LOOKING THIS WAY. DO YOU THINK HE CAN HEAR US?

ARE YOU *CRAZY?* HE'S WAY OVER THERE.

I JUST WISH HE'D STOP *STARING.*

CLARK KENT GIVES ME THE CREEPS.

YOU EVER NOTICE HOW HE ALWAYS JUMPS OUT OF PEOPLE'S WAY? LIKE HE DOESN'T *DARE* BUMP INTO THEM?

HE DOESN'T WANT TO GET SHOVED TO THE GROUND. THE KID'S AFRAID OF GETTING HURT.

HEY!

YOU GOT A *PROBLEM,* KENT?

NO...

IT'S JUST YOU AND ME, *huh?*

TWEET TWEET

HE NEVER LOOKED LIKE *THAT* IN THE HOLO-TAPES, DID HE?

ACTION COMICS #858 VARIANT COVER
ART BY **GARY FRANK**

ACTION COMICS #859 COVER
ART BY GARY FRANK

GOLDEN BOY - KLINT STEWIRT.
HOMEWORLD: EARTH.
ABILITIES: MIDAS TOUCH, SOLID METAL BODY.

SPIDER-GIRL - SUSSA PAKA.
HOMEWORLD: EARTH.
ABILITIES: WEB-LIKE HAIR.

TUSKER - HORACE LAFEAUGH.
HOMEWORLD: EARTH.
ABILITIES: UNBREAKABLE SKELETON.

ACTION COMICS #859 VARIANT COVER
ART BY **ANDY KUBERT**

ACTION COMICS #860 COVER
ART BY GARY FRANK

"COSMIC BOY, LIGHTNING LAD AND SATURN GIRL HELPED US UNCOVER OLD METROPOLIS AND REBUILD IT INTO AN UNDERGROUND SPACEPORT.

"FOR THE LAST SEVERAL MONTHS, WE'VE HELPED BEINGS FROM ALL ACROSS THE UNIVERSE FLEE EARTH. AND WITHOUT EVER HAVING TO GO PLANETSIDE.

"THE STARGATES AT THE FAR END OF THE CITY WERE DESIGNED BY BRAINIAC 5.

"THEY OPEN WORMHOLES THROUGH HYPERSPACE, GIVING US ACCESS TO EVERY SECTOR IN THE UNIVERSE."

WE'VE HELPED OVER TEN THOUSAND EXTRATERRESTRIALS ESCAPE THE ALIEN CONTAINMENT CAMPS AND RETURN HOME.

CAMPS? WE WEREN'T EXACTLY MAKING SNOW CONES AND TELLING GHOST STORIES.

IT'S NICE TO SEE THEY DIDN'T TAKE YOUR SENSE OF HUMOR.

SENSE OF HUMOR WASN'T IN MY ARM.

THIS IS AMAZING, SHADOW LASS.

WE MAKE OUR OWN.

HRFF.

LONG TIME NO SEE, SUPERMAN.

BUT ALL THE POWER THAT'S REQUIRED TO KEEP THIS RUNNING, WOULDN'T SOMEONE NOTICE THAT KIND OF ENERGY BEING SIPHONED OFF?

WE DON'T NEED THEIR ENERGY, KAL.

KRAKKL

LIGHTNING LASS - AYLA RANZZ. HOMEWORLD: WINATH. ABILITIES: ELECTRICAL GENERATION AND DIRECTION.

TIMBER WOLF - BRIN LONDO. HOMEWORLD: ZUUN. ABILITIES: SUPER-HUMAN STRENGTH AND SPEED. HEIGHTENED SENSES AND CLAWS.

WHAT HAPPENED TO THE REST OF THE LEGIONNAIRES?

LIGHTNING LASS AND I MADE IT HERE AFTER HER BROTHER LEFT.

THE FOUNDERS WENT SEARCHING FOR *KRYPTONITE.* PROOF THAT KRYPTON *EXISTED.*

THEY THOUGHT IT MIGHT BE SOMETHIN' TO START SWAYING PUBLIC OPINION BACK OUR WAY.

'COURSE, BRINGING YOU HERE--WE GOT THE *REAL DEAL* NOW.

AW, QUIT KISSING HIS *ASS*, BRIN.

WHAT'S WRONG, WILDFIRE? YOU STILL IN A *BAD MOOD* BECAUSE DAWNSTAR DOESN'T WANT TO PLAY "FIND THE BATTERY" ANYMORE?

RUMORS SAY EARTH-MAN AND HIS CREW BANISHED MON-EL BACK TO THE PHANTOM ZONE. SPIDER-GIRL TRADED WHITE WITCH TO MORDRU IN EXCHANGE FOR HIS STAYING OFF EARTH.

AND CHAMELEON BOY WENT BACK *HOME* TO DURLA TO HELP QUELL THE RIOTS. THE REST...WE DON'T REALLY KNOW.

MIND YOUR OWN BUSINESS, FIDO.

YEP. THE GANG'S GETTING BACK TOGETHER.

YOU HEARD ANY UPDATES ON *OUR* OLD CREW, NIGHT GIRL?

THE STARGATE'S BEEN PROGRAMMED TO WARP US IN ORBIT OUTSIDE OF COLU.

ONCE WE'RE THERE, I'LL BE ABLE TO PICK UP BRAINY'S TRAIL AGAIN.

LET'S HOPE BRAINIAC 5'S ALL RIGHT. WORD IS COLU'S NEW LEADER HAS ORDERED THE *ERADICATION* OF ANY AND ALL BEINGS THAT HAVE COME INTO CONTACT WITH HUMANS.

THE REST OF THE SUBSTITUTES WENT DEEP UNDER AFTER THE JUSTICE LEAGUE PUT DOUBLE-HEADER IN THE GROUND.

RUNNING AWAY?

PLANNING *RETALIATION.*

KAZAAAT

WHO'S THIS NEW LEADER?

YOUR THOUGHTS ARE STRETCHING *MILES* AWAY FROM YOU, LEGIONNAIRES. LEADING ME RIGHT TO YOU LIKE THE SMELL OF A *RED ROSE.*

I HAVE TO REMEMBER TO THANK SATURN GIRL FOR THE *TELEPATHY.*

WE DON'T KNOW, COLOSSAL BOY--

I CAN HEAR YOUR *THOUGHTS,* SHADOW LASS. WISHING MON-EL WAS AT YOUR SIDE.

AND YOU, COLOSSAL BOY, MOURNING FOR YOUR WIFE. THE DIRTY *DURLAN* THAT SHE WAS.

YERA?

ACTION COMICS #860 VARIANT COVER
ART BY **STEVE LIGHTLE**

ACTION COMICS #861 COVER
ART BY GARY FRANK

BRAAL.

EARTH HAS OFFICIALLY SECEDED FROM THE UNITED PLANETS.

AND THEIR *JUSTICE LEAGUE* CONTINUES TO CONDEMN COSMIC BOY AND THE LEGION. THE LEAGUE STILL CLAIMS THEY'VE BEEN SPREADING *LIES* ABOUT *SUPERMAN.*

TITAN.

WE HAVE COME TO EXPECT A CERTAIN LEVEL OF *DISTRUST* FROM HUMANS, BUT NOW THESE XENOPHOBES *DARE* QUESTION SUPERMAN'S KRYPTONIAN HERITAGE?

THEY DO MORE THAN QUESTION IT. THEY ALLOW THE JUSTICE LEAGUE TO PREACH THEIR INSANE GOSPEL--

--THAT SUPERMAN WAS A *HUMAN.* AND THAT HE STOOD AGAINST *ALL* EXTRATERRESTRIALS.

WINATH.

EARTH'S GOVERNMENT HAS BEGUN INCARCERATING *ALL* ALIENS THAT HAVE NOT YET *FLED* THEIR PLANET.

WE *CANNOT* ALLOW THIS BARBARIC TREATMENT OF OUR CITIZENS, OR OUR LEGIONNAIRES, TO CONTINUE.

AS SOON AS COLU DELIVERS THEIR STRIKE PLANS--

I SHOULD'VE *HAD* HIM. SUPERMAN WAS *RIGHT* THERE.

I *HOPE* YOU'RE NOT ENTERTAINING THE IDEA OF FOLLOWING SUPERMAN TO COLU, EARTH-MAN.

THERE'S NO *NEED*, GOLDEN BOY.

I READ TIMBER WOLF'S MIND. THE LEGION IS SEEKING OUT BRAINIAC 5.

BRAINIAC IS *POSING* AS COLU'S LEADER. YET HE'S STILL *ACTING* IN THE INTERESTS OF THE LEGIONNAIRES.

WHAT DO YOU THINK THE COLUANS WILL DO AFTER WE *ANONYMOUSLY* TIP THEM OFF TO THAT?

THEY'LL KILL HIM. THEY'LL KILL SUPERMAN AND THE OTHER LEGIONNAIRES.

AND THE FUTURE WILL *TRULY* BELONG TO THE JUSTICE--

EYEFUL ETHEL - ETHEL LYNN NIWTYN. HOMEWORLD: EARTH. ABILITIES: GROW EXTRA EYES AT WILL.

SPLOK SPLOK SPLOK

WHAT IS IT?

I THOUGHT I SAW...

...NOTHING, BABY. I GUESS IT WAS NOTHING.

IT'S TIME FOR THE NEXT STAGE OF OUR CRUSADE--FIND AND EXECUTE *EVERY* EXTRATERRESTRIAL STILL ON EARTH.

WE HEAD PLANETSIDE IN TWO HOURS.

LONG LIVE HUMANS!

LONG LIVE HUMANS.

GRIFE.

ACTION COMICS #861 VARIANT COVER
ART BY MIKE GRELL

ACTION COMICS #862 COVER
ART BY GARY FRANK

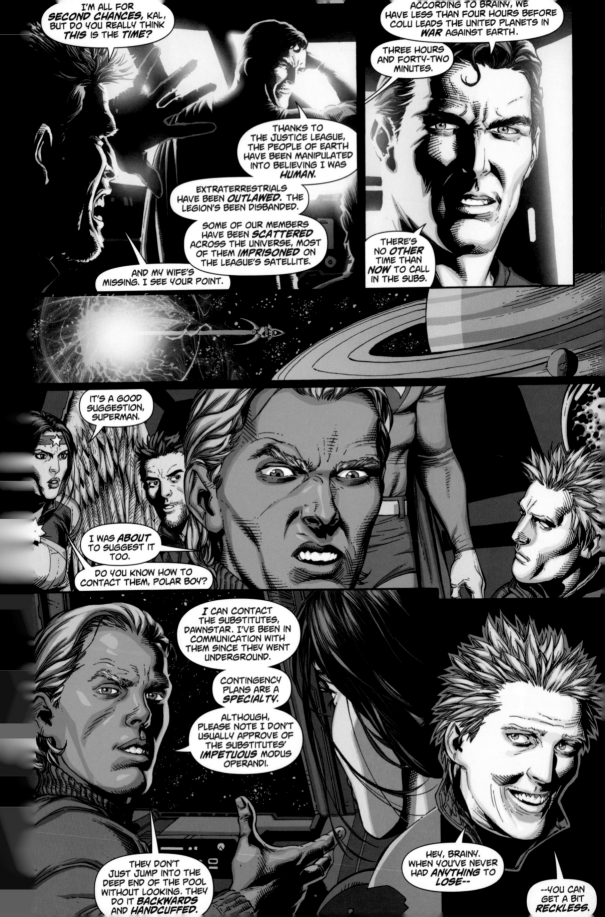

GOLDEN BOY - KLINT STEWIRT.
HOMEWORLD: EARTH.
ABILITIES: MIDAS TOUCH, SOLID METAL BODY.

STORM BOY - MYKE CHYPURZ.
HOMEWORLD: EARTH.
ABILITIES: WEATHER MANIPULATION.

RADIATION ROY - ROY TRAVICH.
HOMEWORLD: EARTH.
ABILITIES: LIVING RADIOACTIVE ISOTOPE.

SPIDER-GIRL - SUSSA PAKA.
HOMEWORLD: EARTH.
ABILITIES: WEB-LIKE HAIR.

NEXT TIME WE HIJACK A SCHOOL BUS, *I'M* DRIVING.

YOU'VE *GOT* TO BE *KIDDING* ME.

...LOOKS LIKE WE WERE **MISINFORMED.**

THE JUSTICE LEAGUE'S **LIES** DIDN'T STOP WITH **YOU,** SUPERMAN. THERE WAS NO "SOLAR SHUTTLE ACCIDENT." EARTH-MAN'S BEEN USING SUN BOY TO **ALTER** THE SUN FROM **YELLOW** TO **RED.**

WE SHUT THIS DOWN, THE SUN GOES YELLOW, AND YOU GET YOUR POWERS--

FORGET MY POWERS. HE LOOKS LIKE HE'S IN **PAIN.**

WE NEED TO GET DIRK **OUT** OF THERE.

I NEED TO SHUT DOWN THIS GENERATOR BEFORE WE UNHOOK HIM.

WE PULL SUN BOY OUT NOW, WHILE THIS MACHINE IS STILL **AMPLIFYING** HIS POWERS, AND HE COULD TRIGGER A **SUPERNOVA.**

TO BE TRUTHFUL, I'M **SHOCKED** HE'S STILL ALIVE. THEY'RE PUSHING HIS SOLAR ABILITIES **FAR** BEYOND HIS NORMAL LIMITS.

GIM?

ACTION COMICS #862 VARIANT COVER
ART BY KEITH GIFFEN AND AL MILGROM

ACTION COMICS #863 COVER
ART BY GARY FRANK

TWENTY-FOUR
HOURS LATER.

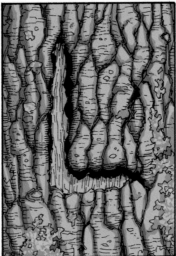

THE END

ACTION COMICS #863 VARIANT COVER

ART BY **GARY FRANK**

FRANK DISCUSSION
A GARY FRANK INTERVIEW

BY TIM PILCHER

Tim Pilcher: The 2007-08 *Superman and the Legion of Super-Heroes* storyline wasn't the first time you'd worked with Geoff Johns, was it? You'd worked together previously at Marvel.

Gary Frank: Yeah, we did a couple of issues of *The Avengers* [#61–62, February 2003], then Geoff left to go to DC and we stayed in touch. I was still exclusive for Marvel for a while, so I was doing some bits and pieces there, and he kept saying, "Come to DC, we've got this going on, it's going to be good." So, when my contract ran down at Marvel, I gave him a call and we talked about what the possibilities were. And it was Superman.

It was odd; because I was never really a massive Superman fan. I always loved the movies, but I never really got into the comics. I think a lot of that is down to, everybody's got that prejudice about Superman being too perfect, etc, and I guess I'd also fallen prey a little bit to that prejudgment. But any character is as good as the writer and as good as the idea that the writer has. So, I talked to Geoff, and with his background with [*Superman* director] Richard Donner [Johns was Donner's production assistant], he was also a big fan of the movies. So, we talked about how much we loved that version of Superman, and how nice it would be to do that as a comic. So that was what swung it for me.

And that was the Legion of Super-Heroes story arc in *Action Comics*?

Yeah, the Legion of Super-Heroes was the first one we did. And then we did the Brainiac arc [*Action Comics* #866–870, August–December 2008]. And then we did *Secret Origin* [2009–10]. And I guess, technically, *Doomsday Clock* [2018–20] is a Superman story as well.

It's kind of funny you saying you weren't a Superman comics fan, as you've done quite a lot of Superman work since!

I think I just didn't give the character enough credit. I kind of had this idea, and it was fixed, and it was only when Geoff said, "It doesn't have to be what you think it is. It doesn't have to be like that..." I used to like Superman as a guest star, I felt he worked like that. You could have de-powered characters, more grounded characters, and you could use Superman as a godlike character. But I didn't really have any hankering to delve into him any further than that, even when he worked as a really humanised character in something like *Kingdom Come*, or something where he's a god, but there's that humanity in it.

I guess there are certain projects which lend themselves to that sort of interpretation; I just didn't have the impression that was the kind of thing which went on in a regular monthly title. So, when I finally got talking to Geoff and he was saying, "You know, he needs to be like this, and he needs to be like that," I was going, "Oh God, yeah, that's right, that's right! That's how he does need to be!" And we got a chance to do that. It was a distillation of all of the things we liked and then thrown together to get a version of Superman that we liked.

You weren't such a Superman fan at that point, but were you a Legion of Super-Heroes fan at all? Did you even know about the Legion?

No, I knew nothing. As a kid, I was the 'Marvel kid'. I would buy *Detective Comics* and DC stuff every now and then, and I bought the essential books like *Dark Knight Returns* and the 'must reads', but I grew up on Marvel. My introduction to comics was the black-

HAIR OR NO ? LOOKS COOL BUT MAYBE TOO ALIEN ?

ABOVE: Gary Frank's character sketches for Braniac 5 and Chameleon Girl.

and-white reprints from Marvel UK. I used to read *Spider-Man Weekly*, and the black-and-white Pocket Books, which was how I got exposed to all the old Kirby and Ditko stuff. Then, in my teenage years, I lost it all and then dipped back into comics after I finished school.

I didn't really know what to do as a career. I remembered this dream I had [of working in comics], which at some point obviously became colossally unrealistic, and so was abandoned. And I remembered that, and just began to dip back into comics. It was that time when *X-Men* was getting big, with Jim Lee, Marc Silvestri, and all of those guys. A really exciting time to jump back in – certainly from an artistic perspective. There were guys like Peter David and Chris Claremont doing these great runs on *The Incredible Hulk* and *The Uncanny X-Men*. And it was a period when, all of a sudden, these superstar artists started arriving – just before everything became all about the art. So, there were still good stories, and there was also this new wave of artists coming through. That was all happening at Marvel. But there was stuff at DC I was also into. I loved Norm Breyfogle's stuff on *Detective Comics*, so I kind of got into that, but a lot of the DC stuff just didn't

resonate with me, in the sense that it wasn't something I was exposed to as a child. So, it wasn't something I necessarily prioritised at that point.

So, I was a Marvel kid, and the Legion didn't really mean anything to me. I mean, I could recognise the main four or five, but I didn't understand why they were so important. But Geoff is a huge, huge Legion fan, a huge DC fan in general, but particularly Legion and the old stuff. He's really of that school. But I was afterwards [too]. I mean, these things don't hang around for 70 years if they're not good ideas. Once you get exposed to them, and have that excuse to delve into them a little bit, you can pick up on why they are, and it tends to be an infectious thing. Most of it depends on where you are when you dip in, and who's holding your hand when they're leading you into it. Geoff and I have got really similar sensibilities

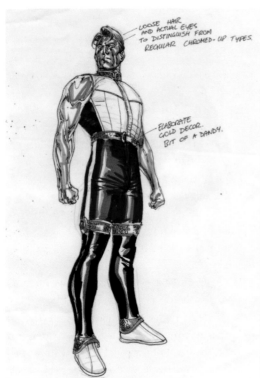

ABOVE: Gary Frank's designs for Golden Boy, Lightning Lass, and, opposite, Night Girl.

in terms of what we like to do with a comic, and what we love about stories. So, if you've got someone saying, "These are great, because…" and they're selling you on an idea and approach they already know you're enthusiastic about anyway, then it's a lot easier to immerse yourself.

Is that the reason why you and Geoff have worked together for so long? Your careers have been pretty much intertwined over the last 20 years.

I know, it's so weird. I guess it's just like the thing of, as you get older, time starts really, really accelerating in horrific and terrifying way. So, I had this feeling that Geoff and I have just been working together for the last few years, and then there was the rest of my career before that. But it's quite terrifying when you realise that so much time has passed in those last few years of my career…

You discovered that you've been working with Geoff longer than you haven't been working with him!

Exactly. We have a very similar approach. We both put storytelling first. We don't like to make anything too splashy – it's all about building a relatable character at the end of the day. How do we make this character somebody you can get to know and feel something for – because otherwise you're drawing 'action figures', right? So, in those quiet moments, between the fights, that's your opportunity to make a connection and bond between the reader and the character, so that when there's a big fight, they care. If the bond isn't strong, there's not so much jeopardy. So, we concentrate on that aspect. The action stuff is there as well, but the important thing is, first and foremost, you need to connect.

And given that is what I like about comics, and what I like to do with comics, that's probably part of why I didn't really understand Superman so much, because it was 'how do you identify with that character?' I know this is a cliché – everybody says it, whether they read comics or don't – but this idea that he's overpowered. The other one is the Clark Kent thing. Is he really Clark Kent, because why wouldn't he be shy and bumbling when he's Superman? Once

I'M THINKING OF KEEPING THE BEEHIVE. WHAT DO YOU THINK?

NOT SURE IF THE CAPE IS RETRO-COOL OR A LITTLE CAMP.

> As Clark Kent, he questions himself. He's not necessarily secure, he tries to imagine what would be the best thing to do for everybody else

you get yourself into the character, those questions disappear, because it just really depends on how well you, or the writer, understands the character.

So, the thing about Clark Kent, for instance, where they say, "Is Clark Kent just a guy he pretends to be so that he can fit in?" Because it's hard to understand that he's so confident, and able to do all of these incredible things, why would he be terrified in a work environment? But it makes complete sense, because there's no correlation between the two situations. What is the type of person that Superman would be if he was in a situation like this? We know he's super-powerful; we know he could wipe out a city; we know he could pick up a person and throw them a mile. How does that help him if he's a complete asshole? The idea that sometimes Superman – because he's so powerful – is going to gain confidence from that

power, that he's going to be able to use it in a social situation, is to colossally misunderstand that hero in the first place. He's not going to be sitting there, cool and confident in his office chair, thinking, "I can handle any situation in here because, if push comes to shove, I can just destroy them with my heat vision." These powers mean nothing in that environment. He's still subject to the same frailties, difficulties, and insecurities as we all are in that kind of environment, because being Superman doesn't give him the tools to deal with that.

You could almost say that Clark Kent is the interior landscape that we all have to deal with.
I think Clark Kent is how a hero would deal with those situations. Superman is the way that a hero would deal with the other type of situation. So as Clark Kent, he questions himself. He's not necessarily secure, he tries to imagine what would be the best thing to do for everybody else, how he can best help people. All of these things are the same kind of basic instincts he has as Superman, it's just that he doesn't have the same tools that he has as Superman. So, all he's got really is decency and humility, and those are the tools that he deploys in that situation.

It's not about conflict resolution through fistfights.
Yeah, exactly. It's about empathy. It's about trying to understand how people can feel good in those situations, and how he can help people feel comfortable.

Geoff has said that your Superman art is the best of your generation, matched only by Curt Swan, which is a quite a nice compliment.
Yeah, that makes me blush! I don't really know what to do with that, but it's really flattering!

When you're drawing Superman, what is your approach? Do you underplay his physicality, or play it up?
It certainly depends on the situation that he's in. Superman would not be above – if it was needed – physically intimidating somebody, but he's not going to go around dealing with every situation in

ABOVE: Frank's design for Radiation Roy, and an unused version of Saturn Girl.

the same way. If you have that much power, it's not necessary to keep on demonstrating it continually. You can relax a little bit and have the confidence that if things happen, you can deal with them, but it's not about shoving your chest in people's faces all day. I'm a big fan of trying to work body language, expressions, and those kind of things into the comic anyway, no matter who the character is. So, for me, a lot of it was that.

There's already a pretty good template in the films – Superman's not the biggest guy in the world. He slips easily between Superman and Clark Kent; you see the change. It's not two completely distinct versions, there's a lot of overlap. There's a famous

[scene] where Lois confronts Clark with the belief that he's Superman, and he's about to tell her, and he straightens up and changes his posture. But there are those steps, and you know what he's thinking about, between those two states; he's going from this humble guy. He certainly overplays it, but there's also a continuity you see in those films, and you see a lot of glimpses of one within the other. So, there's that moment where he slides between the two, which is really nice. Those are the kinds of things that it's nice to put into the comic, even if you don't get a chance to do exactly that sort of thing, but the idea that you can draw him in one situation, and then draw him in another situation

with a completely different posture, or completely different body language.

Obviously, there's an element of Christopher Reeve in my work, and I get asked about that a lot. Before I began drawing Superman, I spent a lot of time looking at those films and sketching expressions just to hardwire them in, along with the way he behaved in certain ways. It wasn't so much that I wanted to reproduce the movie on the page, but I just wanted him to feel like the same character. So, if you're reading a speech balloon, it's that voice that you hear. I don't want to hear a booming superheroic voice, I want that Christopher Reeve baritone coming across, because that's the charming aspect.

When Grant Morrison and Frank Quitely were working on *All-Star Superman*, Grant said something similar – that if you are the most powerful being on the planet, you don't need to be doing all the big postures, because you inherently have that strength. And it feels like you've gone through a similar kind of process, where it's contained and not muscular or showy.
Yeah, yeah. He knows it's there, so he doesn't need to do anything. And the same in terms of the physique; there's no point in giving him huge muscles, because, why? You know that's not where he gets his power from anyway. You don't need to make him look like a steroid monster. He can just look like a reasonably fit, athletic guy who grew up in Kansas on a farm and looked after himself. He should be that kind of thing. There's a little exaggeration, but he's still human looking.

A bit like Spider-Man, that same sort of athletic build, slim but strong.
Yeah, well, my Spider-Man's even skinnier, because I liked Spider-Man as a kid, but I don't very often draw Spider-Man. But yeah, there's the switch where you go from Steve Ditko, where he's a skinny kid, and then over the first few issues of John Romita, suddenly he's becoming Spider-Man.

Throughout your career, you've worked largely with two inkers: Cam Smith in the early years, and latterly Jon Sibal. Your

pencils are incredibly tight, so what do you look for in an inker?
It's different things in different periods. So, with Cam, we both came up together through Marvel UK, and our styles evolved together. The earliest person I really wanted to draw like – my big favourite, and has been consistently throughout my career – is Arthur Adams, even though his style has changed. I really liked that style. And when we were at Marvel UK, Jim Lee and the guys were breaking in, and I just became obsessed with Jim Lee's work. There was also a 'house style' evolving. We'd go into the London offices and there were copies of *X-Men* and stuff around, so it was Jim and Marc Silvestri and that kind of stuff. We were all looking at that, and this was the future. So initially, there was a lot of that shoehorned into my style. And then I started to move away, and I really wanted to clean my stuff up. So, I started looking at people like Alan Davis, thinking I don't need as much line, and [Marvel UK's Editor-in-Chief] Paul Neary was saying that at the same time. And so, because Cam and I were working together, we basically cleaned up the style together, and got a much slicker-looking style.

> Obviously, there's an element of Christopher Reeve in my work, and I get asked about that a lot.

The *Incredible Hulk* stuff was probably the period in which my style, and I assume Cam's, was coming together and firming up the most, because of the quantity of work we were doing. Then, later, there was a stylistic shift again. I got to a point where I was kind of running up against a wall with that super-clean style. I started getting into cleaner and cleaner art, like Steve Rude [*Nexus*, *World's Finest*], and Jaime Hernandez [*Love & Rockets*] was just a god. I really wanted to be able to use that space in the same way those guys were using it. But it became all-consuming and it became hard work, until at some point, I thought, "This is probably not my style. I'm trying so hard to get something as a finished product which looks the way I want it to look, it's not really naturally my style." I was ending up with something

Inside the right image: SPIDER-GIRL

Handwritten note in center: REALLY JUST CHANGES IN THE DETAILING. EARLY VERSION SEEMED TO HAVE GREYISH SKIN. I QUITE LIKE THAT.

ABOVE: Designs for Shadow Lass and Spider-Girl.

which wasn't committed enough to the use of black against white, to make a coherent style, but I was shackling myself by not using textures in order to try to get halfway to where I thought I wanted it to go.

And so, at some point, I just kind of pulled back and said, "I'm just going to start doing different lines and start hatching more and just let the art sort of evolve a little more naturally." So, Jon was good for that as well, because even though he's a hugely technically accomplished inker, he just works better with my slightly more dense style. But then at some point, I just started to enjoy inking my own stuff more than seeing it inked by somebody else.

I'm almost surprised that you've had inkers, because I've seen your pencils and they are insanely tight.

Exactly. When you consider that the whole point of inking originally was to take something, a sketch, that was done in a bullpen, and then hand it over to somebody else to tighten up and finish it – so the penciller could get five or six books per month done – I was achieving nothing, because I was spending the same amount of time doing this stuff with a pencil as

I would have been by inking it. The only difference was the control freak in me was always slightly unsatisfied, because I was always once removed and I could never quite finish the thing exactly. So, I would do an expression on a tiny, little head, and because you're doing little, tiny lines, and they're all slightly rough, it's open to interpretation. And then an inker would ink it and I'd say, "If I could just have that back again, I'd like to tweak that, as it's not exactly the expression I wanted," or something like that. So, there was a frustration.

But what I like to see changed slightly, and I began to enjoy slightly rougher art, where you see the tools on the page. I'm not a particularly accomplished inker, but that's not my goal. I want something that looks organic. The artists that I find myself looking at, and who give me the biggest buzz, are the guys who aren't so mechanically perfectly aligned. I like the organic nature, and the roughness, and the little errors – that stuff feels much more real to me. And it feels like there's some continuity from the art form that I fell in love with as a kid. Maybe it's because now we've gone from a point – within my career – where what I was doing was considered the technological apex of the art form; we couldn't believe we were getting colourists that were getting digital colour, and all of a sudden we could have shades and everything, we weren't having all the old colour separations. So to go from that, to where we are now, where if your goal is to do something perfect-looking you may as well just feed it into a machine, because in a world where there's Pixar, what's the point in trying to have a really perfect comic page? You need to go back in the other direction, and go back to the thing which was different: the idea of a pen or a pencil putting ink on a rough surface. It just feels to me more rich.

You still prefer to work traditionally then, with pencil and paper?

Yeah. You can see some of it in the finished page, but it's not until you go to a show and see a dealer with original pages, and then you see the whiteout and you see all of that. I love that. I hate the idea that is missing from the process. You generally work faster digitally, and certainly the people I've spoken to who have made the jump say that you lose the original art sales, but you become more productive. So, there's a balance to be had.

In terms of production, are you a page-a-day kind of guy? What's your general working process?

I can be, sometimes, it just depends on so much. But yeah, if I've got the script and everything's going OK, and I think that I don't need any reference or anything, I guess I'm about four pages a week, that's a comfortable rate for me. Any more than that and I start to get exhausted, I start to get problems with my hands – cramps and things like that. This is the unfortunate thing about accepting that your style has a lot of lines, they've all got to be drawn! So, there aren't too many shortcuts with that kind of stuff. By relaxing and letting it develop that way, I get something which I'm kind of happy with, but there's a price to be paid in terms of labour.

In terms of how you work now, did you ink all of *Doomsday Clock* yourself?

Yeah.

Did you ink traditionally or did you digitally convert the pencils?

No, no. It was traditional, in the sense that I don't use an inkpot and brushes, I use markers and pens, because I've destroyed so many pieces of artwork by forgetting a piece is not dry. I'm not mentally disciplined enough to be able to work on bits and know which bits I've done and which bits I need to leave alone. I inevitably get into something to an extent where I realise I've just destroyed half of it. These pens dry quickly and they allow me to relax when I'm drawing, which is the important thing. If the goal is to have something which feels organic, you need to be relaxed when you're doing it.

When you were working on *Action Comics*, did you draw the pencils and then courier them to Jon?

Yeah, he's in the States. But that was back in the days when everything had to physically be sent everywhere.

Do you get involved much with the colouring of your work?

BELOW: Design for Storm Boy.

I generally work with Brad Anderson most of the time now. So, unless it's covers or a project that he's not available for, we generally tend to always work together. We've got a pretty good understanding. I know that I can completely relax with him and I can trust him to do his thing. Occasionally, there'll be a story-related point that might need tweaking or something. So, I'm in touch with him. But it just works that way. It's pretty easy. We've now got a little production line going with Geoff, me, Brad, and Rob Leigh doing the lettering. So, we're all in touch with each other all the time when we're getting a book finalised. The only hiccups come when, in terms of busyness, Geoff can be sometimes very occupied with a TV series or something, and Brad is so in demand that he needs to plan weeks in advance when he's going to be able to fit something in, because he's one of the most sought-after colourists in the industry.

> ## The thing about working with Geoff is that he's a very collaborative guy.

Colourists do a lot more 'heavy lifting' in comics these days; do you feel that they're underappreciated?

I don't know. You could go back years ago, to the beginning of the industry, and pencillers were nothing, you know. You had pencillers who didn't have any say. You'd get a guy who'd get a lot of work if maybe he could produce a lot of pages, because then you could get the product out and keep it rolling. I would guess probably the same of writers, to some extent. You may be a writer who created a thing, in which case you would be considered important. But when you've got multiple writers doing different takes on different characters, I don't even know if they were given as much credit as they deserve. And we've now got to a point… and it's only the market which has dictated this; there's not a point at which the comics companies sat up and felt really guilty and said, "You know what? We really should appreciate pencillers more." It just got to a point where the market said, "We like this penciller, or we like this writer, so we will buy

books from that guy." And the publishers make a commercial calculation. They say, "Well, if we want to sell X number of books, we need to get this writer or artist to do it." And that's the way we've gradually achieved and carved out what we've got.

Maybe the next step will be colourists or something. As you say, they're doing a much more important part of the work. I don't know in terms of how they're remunerated, but certainly they're not appreciated as part of the creative process. Who created *Watchmen*? Everybody says 'Alan Moore's *Watchmen*', right? If you're lucky, somebody might say Alan Moore and Dave Gibbons. But whoever says [*Watchmen* colourist] John Higgins? Hopefully it will change. Like I said, it's not a moral question. It's not like one day comics companies said, "We're gonna give this status to this person." It's just that they were forced to by the nature of the market.

Internally, in terms of the way that work is distributed, when you've got a writer who can say, "OK, I'll do this story, if I can have this artist," or if this artist wants to do it, then that pushes some power into the artist. And then if the artist says, "Oh, yeah, I'm interested in doing this, who have you got colouring it?" and they say, "We've got blah, blah," "Ah, yeah, I'm not so interested in this." And then they say, "Well, who would you like?" And then I would say, "Would Brad Anderson be possible?" And then maybe, at that point, that's when the whole cake gets cut a little more evenly.

You've worked on pretty much every big character at both Marvel and DC, and you've done your own writing as well. Where would you like to go next, career-wise, and what sort of things look appealing or interesting for you on the horizon?

The writing thing, I kind of dabbled in, and I've realised that I can think of cool scenarios, but that's just such a tiny little part of writing, the rest is just quite intimidating and a huge amount of work, and it's well outside my comfort zone. But the thing about working with Geoff is that he's a very collaborative guy, so he allows me to kind of get that out of my system. I can suggest cool scenarios, and because he's defining the structure and the bones of it, and doing the hard work – the technical aspects

ABOVE: Designs for Tusker, Timber Wolf, and Polar Boy.

– I can then say, "Well, OK, but imagine how this is going to be on a page visually. I think it would be better if we do it like this." And generally, unless there's a specific reason not to, Geoff will indulge me. So, it gives me enough creative freedom that I don't necessarily feel the need to become a writer. I'm happy just to add my little bit and then concentrate on the thing that I know I do well.

But in terms of where and what characters? Well, I just finished the last arc for the last issue of *Geiger* for Image. After that, we're working on another Image story. And then we're talking about another thing after that. At this point we're enjoying being outside of the DC/Marvel garden, playing around with our own stuff, being free of editorial consideration, and just having that luxury of being able to just roll the dice and see what sticks. There's a mixed metaphor!

I've been doing this for about 30 years, and you get paid a page rate, and you get paid a royalty and everything, but I'm not getting any younger, and I would like to get something out there, which is ours, which is mine, from a creative point of view. I'd like to have something, when I finally put down that pencil, to be able to say, "That's my character, I did that. That was the mark I left, not that run I did on something else." And with pensions being what they are these days, it would be nice if, at the point where I can no longer pick up a pen, I got something that can support me in my dotage. That is a gamble. It's a brave new world, so we'll see how it goes.

With the generation before me, you hear every so often some story about some guy who was a legend when you were growing up, and they can't afford to pay their medical bills now, and somebody's doing a crowdfunding thing. How can it be possible that this person ever finds themselves in that position? But the truth is, that traditionally the big two companies are only interested in you while you're making them money. They don't care. You're a freelancer at the end of the day. When you're not selling the book, you're gone, and somebody else will step in. So you need to plan for yourself. 🄳🄲

IF YOU ENJOYED THE STYLE AND ART IN THIS GRAPHIC NOVEL, YOU MAY BE INTERESTED IN EXPLORING SOME OF THESE BOOKS, TOO.

FURTHER READING

GRAPHIC NOVELS FROM DC COMICS

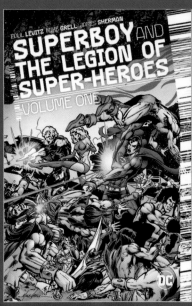

LEGION OF SUPER-HEROES:
THE SILVER AGE OMNIBUS VOL. 1
Otto Binder, Al Plastino and others

SUPERBOY AND THE LEGION OF
SUPER-HEROES VOL. 1
Paul Levitz, Mike Grell and others

LEGION OF 3 WORLDS
(VOL. 4 OF THE DC HEROES & VILLAINS COLLECTION)
Geoff Johns, George Pérez and Joe Prado

THE SINESTRO CORPS WAR VOL. 2
(VOL. 22 OF THE DC HEROES & VILLAINS COLLECTION)
Geoff Johns, Dave Gibbons, Peter J. Tomasi,
Ethan Van Sciver, Ivan Reis and Patrick Gleason